EMBRACE *Yes*

# Embrace Yes

## THE POWER OF SPIRITUAL AFFIRMATION

Martin Lowenthal

**Red Wheel**
Boston, MA / York Beach, ME

First published in 2003 by
Red Wheel/Weiser, LLC
York Beach, ME
With offices at:
368 Congress Street
Boston, MA 02210
www.redwheelweiser.com

*Library of Congress Cataloging-in-Publication Data*
Lowenthal, Martin.
    Embrace yes : the power of spiritual affirmation / Martin Lowenthal.
      p. cm.
    Includes bibliographical references.
    ISBN 1-59003-039-7 (pbk.)
    1. Spiritual life.   I. Title.
  BL624.L673 2003
  291.4'32--dc21

                                2002152830

Quotations by Rabbi Rami M. Shapiro from *Wisdom of the Jewish Sages*, copyright
© 1993 by Rabbi Rami Shapiro, used by permission of Bell Tower, a division of
Random House, Inc.

Rumi translations are from *The Way of Passion* by Andrew Harvey, published by
Frog, Ltd., © 1994 by Andrew Harvey. Reprinted by permission from the publisher.

Typeset in Minion and Scala Sans by Kathleen Wilson Fivel.

Printed in Canada

TCP

10 09 08 07 06 05 04 03
8  7  6  5  4  3  2  1

# Table of Contents

# Acknowledgments

I AM DEEPLY grateful to Jerome Petiprin and to my wife Karen Edwards for their commentary and feedback on the original version of this manuscript. The process of editing this work with Jill Rogers at Red Wheel was both enjoyable and very helpful. I am also thankful to Sonia Baerhuk and Jean Ethier for their support in developing this work and to Donna Blakeman Welch for her comments. I also owe thanks to Annemie Curlin for her assistance with the translation of Rainer Maria Rilke.

I am profoundly grateful to all my teachers. I want to express particular thanks to the late Dilgo Khyentse and to Lopon Tenzin Namdak whose very presence manifests YES in every moment, to Tenzin Wangyal Rinpoche for his unwavering encouragement, and to Lar Short whose creative ways of presenting teachings was an inspiration for the format of this book.

My greatest gratitude embraces the Divine for the gift of life and for the endless teachings that have flowed from that gift.

*Yes*

# Introduction

I INVITE YOU on a journey of affirmation. Affirmation of all that is. This journey takes us to the very heart of the spiritual. By affirming what is, we embrace our aliveness and the conditions of life as presented in the living moment. Our affirmation is not mere positive thinking but the positive power of Presence, Openness and Wonder, Celebration and Service, Love, and Learning and Dedication. Our affirmation, our sense of YES, is of the heart not the head.

I use a number of designations for God, the Divine. Each is intended to address a different aspect of that which cannot be defined, divided, conceptualized, or spoken. I call these aspects the five faces of God:

*God as Reality*—all that is. Reality is God's Presence, always inclusive and complete.

*God as Essence*—beyond and in all that is. The open, unnameable, no-thingness of all that is. Essence is beyond all things and is the nature of everything.

*God as Creation*—the generative force and capacity that makes, preserves, and destroys. Creation is always in process and becoming. It is the power that vitalizes life and radiates in all Reality.

*God as Beloved*—the impulse to connect, care, and make meaning. The Beloved inspires, vitalizes, and connects to us in the very core of our being.

*God as Wisdom*—the clarity that informs all Presence and makes it possible to follow a spiritual path. The recognition, integration, and realization of all aspects of God.

Our overall attitude, way of perceiving, and sense about life, reality, and who we are are our Heart Postures. Our Heart Postures include our self images, compelling concerns, and ways of relating to the world. They include who we unconsciously think we are and what we feel compelled to accept as true about life.

Our Heart Postures are so powerful that they determine our sense of reality in the moment. If we believe that the world is filled with pain, we will see pain in even happy situations. We will project our ideas of pain onto the world. If we believe life is a struggle, we will see the struggle for survival in the world. If you look at anything in nature, most of the time every plant, every tree, every animal simply goes about its life being itself without engaging in the tension of struggle. The struggle for survival is our projection onto nature.

On the other hand, if we believe that everything is interconnected, we will perceive our connections to others. When our Heart Posture is open and loving, we will see beauty and connection in the world.

Each face of God suggests a subtly different Heart Posture of Affirmation. The development and embodiment of each Heart Posture is a path to the experience of communion with the Divine:

The Heart Posture of Yes as *Presence* corresponds to God as Reality.

The Heart Posture of Yes as *Openness* and *Wonder* is associated with God as Essence.

The Heart Posture of YES as *Celebration* and *Service* reflects God as Creation.

The Heart Posture of YES as *Love* relates to God as Beloved.

The Heart Posture of YES as *Learning* and *Dedication* works with God as Wisdom.

This book presents an essential aspect of spiritual work as I have come to experience and teach it. The simple affirmation from our core of YES is both profound and runs contrary to our habitual reactions to much of life. Affirmation, according to the dictionary, is the "confirmation of anything established," whatever is actually so, namely Reality. I invite you to read this book as a kind of meditation, experiencing the subject as you progress. At various points in the text I insert 〰 as a suggestion to pause, experience, and verify the truth of what you have just read. At other times, I will insert *Yes* at the end of a passage to emphasize the point and invite you to sense affirmation in your own being. Whenever you experience recognition, sense the aliveness of your YES.

## Chapter 1

# Yes As Presence
# God As Reality

To attend to creation is to attend to God.
To attend to the moment is to attend to eternity.
To attend to the part is to attend to the whole.
To attend to Reality is to live constructively.
—*Pirke Avot* VI:11 as translated by Rabbi Rami Shapiro

Wherever you turn is God's face.

—Muhammad

## THE HOSTING PRESENCE OF YES

When our Heart Postures are open, fresh, and vibrantly alive, we meet the Presence in nature with our living Presence. With the Heart Posture of YES we see everything just as it is by being just as we are as another living Presence.

The YES of being fully present can include and host everything that is and all that arises. In hosting, our awareness is open and fresh, acknowledging everything. When we host, we are manifesting the Divine as Host, the omnipresent, all inclusive, pure Being. YES as Hosting Presence embraces everything in the home of Presence.

$\sim$

We begin with a short meditation of affirmation.

Take a deep breath and sigh as if you were settling into a pleasantly warm bath, letting your shoulders, neck, and jaw relax. Pause. Take another deep breath and sigh, releasing tensions throughout your body as you read. Pause. Take one more deep breath and once again sigh, saying, "Yes," allowing your body to settle into alert stillness.

Now place your attention in your hands. Simply notice the sensations in your hands and as you witness them, inwardly allow the core of your being to silently say, "Yes." After a short time, you may notice some tingling sensations and pulsing in your hands. Sense the affirmation of this energy of your aliveness as [YES].

Notice that your breathing is settling into a rhythmic pattern and that you can maintain some of your attention in your hands while simultaneously attending to your breathing. Notice that you can also hear sounds.

[YES]

Listen not only with your ears but also with your whole body.

[YES]

Listen particularly from the back of the head where the skull and spine meet.

[Yes]

Have a sense of listening to sounds and to the silence in which the sounds arise.

[Yes]

Notice that thoughts come and go, and feelings arise, pass through, and disappear.

[Yes]

Maintain some of your attention in the sensations in your hands and your breath, some in your listening, and some simply in witnessing your thoughts and feelings. Experience yourself witnessing and hosting sensations, sounds, silence, thoughts, and feelings.

[Yes]

Host everything that arises in the space of your awareness.

[Yes]

Experience yourself as a Hosting Presence.

[Yes]

Sit quietly with your eyes gently open and unfocused, hosting everything that arises and sense Yes in the core of your being. Allow yourself to be just as you are and everything else to be just as it is.

[Yes]

Experience being present. Now.

[Yes]

## Experience of Now

YES is the fundamental affirmation. Affirmation here is not agreement with or liking something. It is simply being present with what is. YES affirms the Divine as Reality, the Now. It is the direct affirmation of what is true now. YES moves us completely into the present moment with a sense of Presence.

YES creates a pause, a gap between thoughts.

YES frees us from attachment and opens us to the present moment, which is a continuous moment. YES also brings alertness to the present. Alertness is the marriage of attention and aliveness. The alertness of YES combines awareness, energy, and a sense of direct relationship with the experience of Now.

## Aliveness

Our bodies are alive. Our sensations are a gateway to the vast aliveness of Presence. We experience it in our hands, our face, our feet, and in all our cells. The Heart Posture of Yes as Presence is the way we relate to ourselves and to the world. It's an attitude toward Reality, a way of understanding and organizing the body/mind around that attitude, and an enriching engagement with life.

The power of Presence includes the power to invest our landscape, our tools, and our activities with spiritual powers. We make the world a temple where people, things, and settings have spiritual relevance.

"What is aliveness?" We intuitively know that the answer is not in chemical and physical definitions of the attributes of life. We sense that it has something to do with experience and the way we relate to experience. Aliveness involves manifesting the energy of life as a way of being and as a Presence in the world that others can experience. It is always fresh.

Aliveness is on the edge. Presence is the connectedness of that edge. Being is the ground that includes the edge and all that is not edge.

In Yes, there is nothing required of us to be alive and complete. We are completely who we are in each moment.

## "No" as Affirmation

In the Hosting Presence of YES, our heart is saying "Yes" to our circumstances, to our feelings, to our actions, to both our likes and dislikes, to our joys, to our tears, and to all the challenges that come with being a participant in a rich, incomprehensible, always changing, and limitless universe.

The embrace of YES includes "No." When we express disagreement, we are affirmatively taking a position. YES is not about agreement. It is about being genuine in our Presence. When we need to say "No" to some request, in our heart we are affirming the act of saying "No" and the setting of boundaries. Our Heart Posture of YES is expressed through "No" as an authentic engagement with others. This transforms boundaries from points of exclusion and negation to points of meeting and affirmation.

## "Yes" and YES

There are many types of "yes." There is the "yyyesss!!!" of pumped excitement and achievement. At these times, what is true in the world matches our hopes. We have just been awarded grand prize in an art competition. We sank a basket from midcourt. We changed the mind of a committee through our eloquence and logic. This "yes" is a conditional embrace of the present. Things might have come out differently and our response could have easily been denial and rejection.

The "yes" of agreement is entirely conditional on whether we like an outcome or a statement. This simply confirms our position on some matter. We may embrace the result, and our acceptance is dependent on our attitude and opinion. This "yes" comes from our thinking and feelings.

The YES from our core is unconditional and is simply our aliveness meeting the aliveness of the world. This YES can include our agreements and disagreements, our likes and dislikes. YES includes judgment and is nonjudgmental. YES accepts that we have our position on issues and others have their positions.

## Comforting Reverie

The "yes" of reverie is a wholehearted embrace of what is remembered or imagined. One of the most striking examples of this in literature is the ending of the classic *Ulysses* by James Joyce:

> O and the sea the sea crimson sometimes like fire and the glorious sunsets and the figtrees in the Alameda gardens yes and all the queer little streets and pink and blue and yellow houses and the rose gardens and the jessamine and geraniums and cactuses and Gibraltar as a girl where I was a Glower of the mountain yes when I put the rose in my hair like the Andalusian girls used or shall I wear a red yes and how he kissed me under the Moorish wall and I thought well as well him as another and then I asked him with my eyes to ask again yes and then he asked me would I yes to say yes my mountain flower and first I put my arms around him yes and drew him down to me so he could feel my breasts all perfume yes and his heart was going like mad and yes I said yes I will Yes.

## Completeness

YES brings us into a direct, intimate relationship with others, the world, and life. One of the most prevalent barriers to this intimate relationship is the habitual orientation that life is inherently problematic. When we think or feel that life is a problem or filled with problems, a deep sense of separation and dis-ease resides in the soul. Denial, suffering, and longing become our way of relating and make us a prisoner of dissatisfactions and demands. Our bodies are designed to experience aliveness and connection, not isolation and alienation.

~

The path to freedom from this prison is not the loss of individual consciousness, nor finding solutions to our problems, nor the dissolution in some cosmic oneness. The path is learning to see all things as complete in this very moment and to meet that completeness with our Presence.

YES is not the solution to the problems of our lives. YES is the aliveness of presence beyond the problem frame of mind. In YES there are no problems, there is simply "what is."

### Presence Simply Is

To understand the completeness of YES, we may consider incomplete space. Can such a phenomenon be conceived? Try to imagine defective atoms and molecules. Such things can only make sense when we have some idea of how we would like them to be different. Atoms and molecules simply are what they are. The entire physical world is simply what it is.

Physically, we are composed of space and atomic particles. All of us have the same physical ingredients. We may be different combinations but the space and particles of everybody else are no different from ours.

We are simply "who we are," no matter what we or others think or feel about it. Our presence in the world is neither good nor bad, flawless nor flawed. It simply is.

## Open to Aliveness

When we are not clouded by expectation, shaded by disappointment and discomfort, and fragmented by denial and resistance, we can experience the open, luminous, and complete nature of aliveness.

There is a large oak outside my window. It needs no validation, approval, or change. This oak is still a tree even after a recent ice storm broke some branches. The tree does not have an attitude about that fact. It simply is.

Each morning the tree presents itself to my attention without reservation. Each moment of our meeting is fresh, vivid, and alive. Nothing is needed and nothing needs to be taken away.

*Yes*

## LIFE IN DENIAL: THE REACTIVE HABIT BODY

When we deny the living Presence of all that is, we set up a life in denial. To be ignorant is to ignore Reality. To ignore Reality is to ignore God.

When we react from fear, desire, and confusion, we become self-concerned, self-preoccupied, excluding the world as it is. We shut out the Divine as Reality. In this denial we become separate from Reality and long to bridge the distance between us and life. The loss of intimacy alienates us from God.

In the affirmation of YES we take our place in the world, being fully present in the moment.

*Becoming Whole*

"God's presence is the fullness of the world."

—Isaiah 6:3

In a life of denial we feel out of place. We search for how we fit, for our belonging. How does our piece fit into the puzzle of life? As a piece in the Divine picture, we long to find our place in the whole where our boundaries and limitations disappear.

In YES all life is equal. Everything is a part of Reality. We are another piece along with the elephant and the ant. Each has its place. We have ours. When we know our place as a part, the entire picture becomes clear and we become whole.

Judah ben Tema used to say:

One who hardens his face against the world
is trapped within the self,
closed to Reality,
and lost in a land of
exiled selves and selfishness.

One who softens her face before the world
forgets the self,
is open to Reality,
and creates a world of compassion and peace,
where each is a part of everyone
and everyone a part of all.

—*Pirke Avot* V:24 as translated by Rabbi Rami Shapiro

If we are not consciously present in the world and do not allow Reality to inform us about who we are and where we belong, we will never know where we uniquely belong. YES is the realization that the Divine, as complete Reality, manifests in everything, in all the finite pieces.

## Cut Off from God

When we identify with our body, our ideas, and our feelings, we set the stage for feeling threatened, needy, and wounded by physical pain, disagreement, and emotional discomfort. These identifications are erroneous ideas about who we are. They are vanities, and they require protection, care, and satisfaction. These requirements in turn place us in an ongoing struggle with the flow of life and lead to a sense of suffering. The sense of struggle and suffering cuts us off from our Presence, forming patterns of denial of Reality.

In the Old Testament the lower world of hell is called "sheol," which is the realm of diminishing being. This is the bleakness of the Bible, referred to in Deuteronomy 33 as the choice between life and death. As Jacob Needleman says:

> Sheol is the condition of human life proceeding with ever diminishing human presence. It is the movement toward absence, the movement away from God—for let us carefully note that one of the central definitions of God that is given in the Old Testament is conscious presence. Moses asks God, "What shall I say to the people of Israel? Whom shall I say has sent me with these commandments?" The answer he receives, as mysterious today as it has ever been: "Say unto the children of Israel, I AM has sent me unto you." (Exodus 3:14)

## Hostage to Fears

When we are totally preoccupied and run by the sensory world, we lose the sense of the greater Presence, which is the sacred. We lose perspective and relate everything to our personal story. We lose the source of enduring meaning, love, and satisfaction.

If we look deeply at our everyday reactive habits, we will see fear and longing lurking in much of what we do, haunting how we move, what we say, our posture, our tone of voice, our actions, our drives, our accomplishments, our failures, our boredom, our relief, and our joys.

When we let our deepest fears guide our actions, our relationships, and our way of being, we are hostage to those fears. Our soul cries out for aliveness and lived experience rather than safety and emotional survival. At heart, we do not want our gravestone to read, "Here lies _____, who succeeded for his or her entire life in avoiding what he or she feared would happen and shrank from finding out what he or she most feared to know."

## Clarity

There are points in life when we wonder whether all the assumptions we make about ourselves and the world are really true and whether we devote our lives to what is important. These times are opportunities for pause, for reflecting on patterns, for interrupting patterns, and through a disciplined process of self-observation, realizing we are not our patterns, our quests, our concerns, or our achievements. At these junctures, we can grow by examining our lives and developing an awareness that goes beyond our habitual struggles.

We use our capacity of mind to look at the crystallizations that the mind has created and that the body manifests. We cut through the mental fabrications like a precise laser beam revealing the core of aliveness. We witness all our crystallizations, fixations, wounds, and quests with a sense of Hosting Presence, using their intensity to motivate us in our practice of Presence. We greet each revelation with YES, not judging, denying, or glorifying it.

Our clarity is the clarity of Presence, not understanding. Our maturity is our ability to be inclusive and to relate to everything that we experience as a manifestation of our aliveness. Through the uncompromising discipline of the Hosting Presence of YES, we can discover that none of our reactive habits and compelling concerns has any inherent reality or truth.

## Compassion

Working with our own reactive habits and denial of life provides the base for developing our compassion. Compassion as an experience, a quality of being, and a way of relating to others is also part of the human design. The potential for compassion is developed and matured through the process of living, struggle, and awareness. Through our experiences, we can know something about human experience, and as compassion develops so does the sense of connection and bonding to others and to humanity. Our capacity to relate wholeheartedly grows. We embrace more and more with our YES.

Our transcendence of self-concern in YES and in compassion reveals the radiance of the three jewels of participation, contribution, and consciousness. Our existence takes on a different look and feel as we understand that nothing more is needed and that showing up is participating in the process of life. All actions are realized as contributions and the question becomes, "What is the nature and impact of our contributions?" We realize that we are the environment that others experience, and we can decide to give direction to the ways in which we show up. The YES of our Presence can invite others to relax into the YES of their own Presence.

## GETTING TO YES THROUGH
## OUR PAIN AND ADDICTION

A life spent in denial of Reality embeds us in reactive habits of pain and addiction. For instance, when we do not acknowledge our feelings, we may reactively eat for comfort. Not facing tensions in a relationship can lead to fear of arguments or anger at disagreements. Seeking escape from the discomforts of life may trap us in patterns of drinking, drugs, or compulsive sexual activity.

The deeper, more core sense of self notices our suffering and compulsive behavior. This is not the part of us that judges everything we observe and mentally comments in ways that leave us feeling diminished and anguished. The intimate witness simply notices, moving from each experience to the next without comment, attachment, rejection, or attitude. The intimate witness is present with everything that arises. It brings us into Presence with the reality of our experiences, our actions, our thoughts, and the world. Through intimate witnessing, we can access our Hosting Presence and the sense of YES.

~

In everyday life we act as though our reactive, habitual ideas are real. We react to family and friends as if we know who they are and what they are likely to say and do. The sword of our attention as intimate witness cuts through this shroud of assumed reality and helps us look freshly at situations, people, things—and, of course, ourselves. When we Host our sensations, thoughts, feelings, emotions, and the sounds around us, we rest in an ever-present layer of awareness. Our conscious work with YES as a Hosting Presence brings the clarity of this awareness to the reactive patterns of our habit body as well as simply being present with each habit.

The task is not to rid ourselves of those parts that produce painful feelings and undesirable behaviors. It is not to exorcise some demonic element within, but to recognize that all of these feelings are energies of our aliveness seeking expression and wanting to accomplish something on behalf of our being, in the service of our soul.

In other words, we do not renounce our sensory life—the life of the body, emotions, and mind—but rather notice how we make ourselves unhappy and get stuck in reactive habits. By examining our experience as it is happening, with the quality of affirmative Presence, we reveal not only the structure and nature of those habits of mind, but also the deeper nature or context within which all these phenomena arise. We also discover how the process of thinking and feeling arises, operates, and dissolves.

As we penetrate the surface reactions, getting to the underlying structure of fears and longings, we expose the entire system of archaic beliefs to authentic Presence. We allow all our reactive fears and angers to emerge in the context of our Hosting Presence as well as all the qualities of love, peace, and generosity that make up our fundamental wisdom nature. This wisdom nature resonates as a core truth about what our life really wants to express and manifest. These qualities of aliveness are worth cultivating and are the gifts of Presence we want to bring to the world.

For example, when a friend says to me, "I am disappointed by what you just did," my first reaction may be to become angry and try to explain and justify what I have done. This is my reactive habit body.

If I examine my response more closely, I see that my anger, which seems so real and appropriate, is a defensive reaction based on a chain of fears. These may range from the fear of being judged as stupid, to feeling alone, to feeling that I am not good enough, to feeling that I could die without any support, cut off from everyone who matters. As I look at these fears, I realize that they may not make intellectual sense, but they feel true and thus I attribute "reality" to them as threats.

In my efforts to explain my actions, I see that I have a longing to be understood. I hope that, if others understand me, I will feel connected. I realize that my longing for connection and belonging seems like the solution to the problem of my fears.

Continuing my inquiry, I see that these fears and longings are projections and assumptions I bring to situations and are not inherently there. I understand that they arise out of reactive impulses rather than true perceptions of reality. From this space of not knowing, I pursue the inquiry to find a ground that would allow me to encounter the world more openly and honestly. This requires that I continue to strip away the layers of conceptual identities, emotions, and reactive ideas that all depend on whether I like or dislike the events of my life.

Finally, I arrive at a state that is open, unconditional, and can host all ideas, feelings, and events but is not caused by them. My attention can rest in that sacred dimension of awareness, which is like a mirror, unaltered by the images reflected in it. In this state, I am resting in my wisdom nature.

From this sense of being grounded in wisdom nature, I can now listen to my friend's statement of disappointment with a sense of connection to her, of caring for her, and a sense that we are having a living encounter. Now there is aliveness, energy, and the possibility of deepening our manifest connection. I can relate to the other person not simply through my reactive emotions but with the sense of being fully present with her. Our relationship becomes free rather than defensive, open rather than needy, and authentic rather than pretentious.

*Yes*

## Discovery Through Fear

As reactive habits, emotional reactions, and compulsive thoughts arise in daily life, greet them with YES. Allow your being to say "yes" to each experience, thought, and feeling. Our YES connects us directly with what is actually occurring now. We are intimate with our current situation, experiences, feelings, thoughts, and sensations. This intimate relationship is immediate and direct. We become intimate with Reality.

~

The point is not to get rid of our fears but to show up with all that we are, including the long-lost parts that seek expression through our fears. Fears are distress flares sent into an overcast sky. Fears wait for a truly attentive mind to penetrate the fog and discover the shipwrecked beings of our soul, whose vibrant presence finally brings clear light to what had been endless haze. Through the inquiry process of discovering our wisdom Presence, we come to know where to find the realm of joy, peace, and freedom.

## *Energy of Aliveness*

The trapped energy—the charge—of our reactive emotions is drawn into our sense of Presence when we meet our experiences and the world with YES. We reclaim this energy of aliveness in the very process of making an intimate relationship with Reality.

When we experience anger, for example, our entire body and sense of being becomes alert, focused, and energized. However, the life force of anger is either directed out at others or inward at ourselves. We experience only the anger not our own presence. The energy is wasted.

If we are consciously present and meeting both the world and our intense feelings with a sense of our own presence, we then experience how alive we feel. We can then separate this sense of aliveness from the thoughts that made us angry. The energy of Now enhances our sense of Presence in an open and connected way.

## Wholeness

We experience wholeness in the intimacy of our relationship with Reality—wholeness within ourselves, in our relationship with life, and with the world. By attending to Reality through Yes, we are mindful of the completeness and inter-being of everything in the moment of Now.

All feelings, including conflicting impulses and desires, are included in the space of our hosting awareness and held by our unconditional affirmation in Yes. Nothing is left out or excluded. The wholeness that already exists becomes evident and embraced by our sense of Presence.

When we are present in Yes, other human beings and the rest of nature become wonderfully and completely real to us. True relationship arises when Presencing occurs. In the Yes of Presence we both open to the pain of others and can see beyond that pain to their own radiant being.

When we are fully present with the suffering of others, their pains, joys, and aliveness touch our hearts and break us open. Including the reality and livingness of others in our hearts expresses our interconnectedness. The boundaries between self and other become permeable, allowing the conditions of others in and our caring energies out.

## Rebirth in Aliveness

We die and are reborn in this practice of YES as Presence. We face our deepest fears, our most addictive habits, and our most compulsive wants. These elements of our reactive habit body of denial have kept us from the experience of living life as it is. They shroud us in a kind of death, even as we are haunted by the fear of death. YES takes us into death with the Presence of aliveness. In the process, our reactive habit body dies and we are reborn into our authentic aliveness.

We now inhabit our body more fully, feel our emotions without resistance, see others for who they are, and experience being engaged and connected. It is similar to the catharsis we can feel at the conclusion of an intense bout of the flu. When we recover, we feel fresh and delighted in our own vitality. Our aliveness wants to get out in the world and to dance.

## Just Don't Know

Life is filled with complexity, ambiguity, conflicting feelings and desires, and paradox. There is always more going on than we can know and think about. The actions of others and of the larger forces in society are beyond our control and comprehension. The right course of action is often not clear. We have feelings of love, sadness, anger, and fear in relation to the same person. We want to be closer and more independent. We want to make more money, work less, go out with friends, do more spiritual practice, and spend more time with family. We want more than the limitations of the world and life permit.

The path of Yes as Presence does not try to understand and resolve all these phenomena, options, and desires. Rather we simply affirm that they are all true. We affirm the unknown and not knowing. We affirm all actions and forces even those we cannot control or understand. We affirm our confusion. We affirm that we have many different feelings and that we are not consistent. We affirm all the various desires of what we want as simply what is true about our desires. We meet all these with Yes. In that meeting, everything then feeds our sense of Presence and intensifies our aliveness. This affirmation through Presence can mend the tear we feel in our relationship with life, the world, and God.

## The Great Fixer: A Hasidic Tale

In the Kabbalah of the Jewish tradition, the soul is not something that needs curing from some affliction so much as needing to be repaired, *tikkun*. This is not only the soul of the individual but that of the world, *Tikkun haOlam*. This story is based on the idea that repairing the soul by mending the tear in our relationship to the aliveness of the Divine Presence is the way to supreme joy. Suffering and sorrow comes when we think that life is a problem and unfixable, when we have forgotten the "I am," the Divine Presence in each moment. It is said that if one person truly knew how to fix the soul by celebrating the Divine Presence in life, then that person would repair the whole world. This version is an adaptation of a story told by Rabbi Shlomo Carlbach and included in the book *Shlomo's Stories*.

~

The reigning Monarch of the World, the King of Suffering, wanted to see if the world was still in good shape—that is, if everybody in his realm was sad, fearful, and dissatisfied. For, as you know, what makes a sad person happy is to meet others who are sad. This gives them at least some satisfaction.

So the King of Suffering, disguised in the clothing of an ordinary person, walked all over the world and came back to the city of his palace with deep satisfaction. The entire world was miserable. He had not met one happy, fully present, and peaceful person.

But as he approached his palace, the most horrible sound greeted his ears. The sound of genuine celebration and praise. He traced where the sound came from and found a small shack that was falling apart. He went closer and peered through the window and saw a man sitting at a table with his wife. The table had a simple meal of a few fruits and vegetables, some bread, and a bit of wine to drink. As the couple sipped the wine and tasted the fruits, the man rejoiced in song. There was no doubt that this poor person was happy and serene.

This could mean the end of my kingdom, thought the King, knowing that true happiness is contagious. The King decided to investigate this situation himself since he did not trust any spies or assistants in such an infectious situation.

Still in disguise, the King knocked on the door, and when the man asked who it was, he told him that he was a wanderer, and asked if he might be accepted as a guest. The man immediately opened the door and invited the wanderer to join them to share what little food they had. Then he resumed his joyful celebration. After a while the King said, "My friend. That is quite some song you are singing. Who are you?"

"I am a simple, poor Jew and I am a Fixer! I can repair anything. I wander the streets of the world and announce, 'I am a Fixer! Is anything broken in your home? Bring me your broken hearts, your broken lives! Bring me your broken world. I'll mend it for you. It won't cost you much. Just a few pennies—enough to buy myself a small feast. Because we must have something to eat and offer in our celebration and our praising of the Divine.'"

The King was nervous. Suffering people don't really celebrate. They shovel food down their throats like addicts. They miss the taste. They don't give real thanks and praise for God's gift of aliveness. Only happy people do that. Only they celebrate and experience the transcendent joy of their everyday meals as a feast at God's table.

The King knew he had to test this man and show him the path of suffering. He returned to his palace and prepared a proclamation. The next day when the Fixer walked the streets of the world and began to announce, "I am the Fixer! Bring me...," the people opened their windows and cried out, "Shhh! Didn't you hear? The King made a new decree! No more fixing!"

What a terrible situation! The Fixer was out of a job. He knew he needed to earn something in order to have his feast to celebrate and praise. So the Fixer wandered through the streets of the world sure that something would turn up. He came upon a well-dressed woman carrying water. He thought to himself, "I can do that. From now on I will be a water carrier." So he went to the market and bought a water jug, filled it with water from the central well, announced he had water, and found people who would pay a few pennies for him to bring them water. By the time evening came, he found that he had as much money as usual, which was enough for his wife and himself.

That night the King, again disguised as a wanderer, returned to the shack of the Fixer to see how he was faring after the order he had given. The King was astonished to once again hear rejoicing and to see that the man and his wife were as happy as ever. He knocked and was invited in to share in the feast and celebration. The King asked about the man's day and was told the entire story and the good fortune that came of everything. "The King closed one door," said the man reflectively, "and life opened another."

The King was understandably distressed and excused himself to hurry back to court and make another proclamation. The next day, when the Fixer returned to the well, he discovered that his occupation had been outlawed by the King. Again he was out of a job. He looked around and saw some woodcutters passing by and asked if he could join them. They said, "Sure!" for they could use more hands. So the Fixer cut wood all day, and when they all returned to town and sold the wood they had cut, the Fixer found that he had earned as much from cutting wood as he had from carrying water and repairing what is broken.

Of course, dear friend, you can guess what happened next. That's right. The King came around that evening to find the Fixer and his wife rejoicing and was invited for dinner and told of the day's events.

And yes, you know what the next part of the story is. The King banned woodcutting and the Fixer found something else. The Fixer and his wife would celebrate and praise, the King would visit, find out what the Fixer did each day to earn his feast, and then outlaw that occupation. There were decrees against washing floors, lifting stones, baking bread, collecting garbage, and delivering mail. He even forbade cleaning out public toilets. Whatever service the Fixer found to do, the King took away until the entire kingdom was falling apart and stinking. And people suffered even more.

Now the King, who was frustrated that the Fixer always found something to do to earn his feast and have his celebration, decided on another course. He sent the captain of his guard to where he knew the Fixer would be looking for work. The captain was ordered to draft the Fixer into the palace guard. The Fixer was outfitted with a new uniform and a bright sword, that he never intended to use, being the peaceful soul that he was. He stood guard all day at the palace. When he went to the captain for his wages at the end of the day, he was informed that guards only received their wages at the end of each month and that he would be paid in thirty days. He couldn't convince the captain to loan him even two pennies.

The Fixer and his wife needed to have their feast and celebration because he knew that as long as there's at least one or two people in the world who keep the joy of the Divine Presence alive, there is the possibility of everyone realizing happiness.

So leave it to the Fixer to fix everything. On his way home, he chanced upon a pawn shop, marched in, and sold his sword. He made enough money to live for a year. Then he fashioned a new sword out of wood and put it into the sheath. On his way home he bought some fruit, vegetables, bread, and wine for the nightly feast and celebration.

What a surprise it was for the King that night when he came by and found the couple celebrating and praising the Divine. The King asked the man about his day and received the whole story. When the King asked him what he would do if the King discovered the fake sword and imposed the punishment of death, the man replied, "I am not going to worry right now about things that haven't happened. I will find a way or I won't. I am celebrating now."

The King couldn't sleep that night as he figured out a way to finally trap the Fixer. The next day when the palace guards came to their posts, the King ordered that they report to the civic center. There was to be an execution that day, and it was the custom for all citizens of the world of suffering and sorrow to witness the sentence being carried out.

At the appointed time, everyone assembled as the execution was about to take place. The King, dressed up in his royal attire, strutted up to the Fixer and said to him, "I, the King of the World, appoint you to use your sword and cut off the head of this man, condemned for stealing a melon from the palace garden."

Leave it to the Fixer not to get upset. "With all due respect, your highness, I have never even killed a fly. Do not insist on this execution."

The King started yelling like an enraged bull. "Are you going to defy your King?" He started to choke on his own words. "If you don't carry out the order to execute this man, you will be killed right now!"

Friends, only confused and suffering people are afraid of everyone else. If you are connected to the true Presence, you remain calm.

So the Fixer turned to the assembled throng. He praised the Divine and said to everyone, "You all know me, and the Lord knows me, as the Fixer and that I would never kill an innocent person. I repair what is broken in your hearts and your lives. I have an unbreakable connection to God and so I know that when a man is guilty," (he put his hand on the hilt of his sword) "my sword is a sword that will kill. But when a man is innocent, then my sword turns to wood in my hand."

34

He unsheathed his sword and waved the wooden facsimile in the air. And when everyone saw that it was wooden, the crowd gasped, then clapped and then cheered and rejoiced.

And so the Kingdom of Suffering and Sorrow began to crumble. Even the King was duly impressed. He hired the Fixer as his prime minister and asked him to transform the kingdom.

And that night, everyone feasted and celebrated and sang songs of praise for the gift of aliveness and the treasures of the Divine.

*Chapter 2*

# YES As Openness and Wonder
# God As Essence

Your true nature is not lost in moments of delusion, nor is it gained at the moment of enlightenment. It was never born and can never die. It shines through the whole universe, filling emptiness, one with emptiness. It is without time or space, and has no passions, actions, ignorance, or knowledge. In it there are no things, no people, and no buddhas; it contains not the smallest hairbreadth of anything that exists objectively; it depends on nothing and is attached to nothing. It is all-pervading, radiant beauty; absolute reality, self-existent, and uncreated. How then can you doubt that the Buddha has no mouth to speak with and nothing to teach, or that the truth is learned without learning, for who is there to learn? It is a jewel beyond all price.

—Huang-po

The Nature of Being is beyond defining.
Words are relative and cannot convey what is beyond
conceiving.
Heaven and earth arose within the unknown
unnameable beyond.
Presence is the mother of matter,
And Naming is the womb of all distinctions.
With boundless Openness we realize the hidden
core of life.
In passionate Presence we engage manifestations.
Although referred to differently, the core and the
manifest
Are the same in Essence.
Wonder connects to them both:
From wonder into wonder
The gateway to Wisdom opens.

—Lao Tsu, *The Way of Life (Tao Te Ching)*
as translated by M.L.

## Beyond Here And Now

The Divine as Essence is the intrinsic nature of all Being, becoming, and all that is. Essence is both fundamentally open and always manifesting. The Divine as Essence is referred to as the Godhead, Spirit, the Tao, Natural Mind, Pure Being, and *Ein Sof* (in Kabbalah).

The openness that it takes to be authentically present takes us beyond our ideas about what it means to be here, now. Struggling to be present can trap us in our ideas about what it means to be beyond concepts, beyond time, and beyond our usual experiences. Ideas about openness are like clouds in the sky. They appear to have substance but really obscure our vision of the true open nature of the sky itself.

Relaxing our attention and simply hosting all that arises enables us to contact the subtle space beyond our concepts and efforts. In that relaxation the boundless space of all being opens us to awesome wonder.

> The eyes that regard God are also the eyes through which God regards the world.
>
> —Traditional Sufi Saying

## Beyond Imagination

We can try to imagine the Divine as Essence as boundless space. Yet boundless space is infinite, beyond imagination. The Divine as Essence is beyond boundless space, beyond infinity, and thus beyond imagination. What is beyond infinity is also beyond words. This is what we are referring to by God as Essence.

> It is God, Unique,
> God the Ultimate.
>
> God does not reproduce
> and is not reproduced.
>
> And there is nothing at all
> equivalent to God.
>
> —from the Koran

The fact that we cannot understand, conceive of, or articulate Essence does not mean we cannot know Essence. This knowing is not of the mind as intellect but of the heart that is awake. The Heart Posture of Openness and Wonder is the key to the wisdom of Essence.

The Divine as Essence is paradoxically both transcendent and immanent—transcendent because it is *beyond* everything, immanent because it manifests as everything. The transcendent nature of Essence is powerfully conveyed in one of the most famous Buddhist teaching texts, the *Heart of Profound Wisdom Sutra* (also known as the *Heart Sutra*). It deals with the open, empty, and impermanent nature of all phenomena. This Sutra has many levels of meaning, and the following is one of my interpretative versions that emphasizes the transcendent nature of the Divine as Essence and the relationship of this nature to Presence.

*The Sutra of the Heart of Profound Wisdom*

> Homage to Profound Wisdom, the Beautiful, and the
> Sacred.
>
> One who wishes to practice the profoundest wisdom
> should see in this way: seeing all aspects of
> existence to be without inherent qualities and
> fundamentally open.
>
> Presence is open and this very openness is Presence.
> Whatever is opening is presencing and whatever is
> presencing is opening.
>
> The same is true of feelings, perceptions, impulses,
> and consciousness.
>
> Thus all experiences are open and always opening.
> Openness is beyond characteristics and therefore
> has no inherent characteristics.
>
> Opening is beyond birth and cessation.
> It is beyond impurity and purity.
> It does not decrease or increase.
> Therefore openness is beyond form,
> > beyond feeling, perception, formation,
> > consciousness;
> > it is beyond eye, ear, nose, tongue,
> > beyond body and mind;
> > beyond appearance, sound, smell, taste, touch,
> > beyond experience;
> > beyond the dynamics of sight,
> > beyond mind dynamics and consciousness
> > dynamics;
> > beyond ignorance and end of ignorance,
> > beyond old age and death, and beyond end of old
> > age and death;
> > beyond suffering,

and beyond origin and cessation of suffering;
beyond path and wisdom,
beyond attainment and nonattainment.

Therefore, since there is nothing to be attained, dedicated wisdom beings abiding by means of the Perfection of Wisdom have clarity of mind. They live beyond their fears. They transcend confused reactivity and attain complete realization of their open wisdom nature.

All those who appear as buddhas in the past, present, and future fully awaken to unsurpassable, true complete enlightenment by relying on the Perfection of Wisdom. Therefore one should know the Perfection of Wisdom as the great Teaching, the Teaching of great knowledge and understanding, the utmost Teaching, the unequalled Teaching, allayer of all suffering. In Truth there is no self-deception. Therefore, use the mantra of all-encompassing wisdom:

*Om gate gate paragate parasamgate bodhi svaha*

*Going, gone, having gone beyond, having gone
    completely beyond to the totality, O what an
    awakening, all hail.*

*Om gate gate paragate parasamgate bodhi svaha*

*Pure Presence is transcending,
ever transcending,
transcending transcendence,
transcending even the transcendence of transcendence,
it is total awakeness. It is Suchness.*

## Immanence

In addition to the previous version of the Heart Sutra emphasizing the transcendent nature of the Divine as Essence, I have written an affirmation sutra celebrating the immanent and inclusive nature of the Divine as Essence and the Divine as Reality. By affirming and including everything, we again transcend each particular and arrive at the beyond. We are carried by our affirmation to a profound sense of wonder and gratitude for the openness that holds and hosts all things, all changes, all possibilities.

I humbly offer this sutra to the world and to the great teachers whose wisdom energies inform all wisdom seekers, whose love of all life transcends all judgments, and who challenge us to embrace all that is. May this be of benefit to all and lead swiftly to the happiness, growth, and freedom of all beings.

## The Affirmation of Profound Wisdom Presence: The Yes! Sutra

Homage to the Perfection of Wisdom Presence, the Beautiful, and the Sacred.

Dedicated students of Wisdom
perceive that we are completely surrounded by and filled with Presence manifesting Essence beyond attribution,
open to the all inclusive, totally open Essence and rejoice
in all manifestation in Presence,
live in constant opening and forming.
As students of Wisdom we aspire
to be present in each moment of our feelings, perceptions, impulses, and thoughts and
to celebrate the gift of life and all existence with boundless wonder and resounding joy.

In our lives there is birth and death, Yes.
There is impurity and purity, Yes.
There is decrease and increase, Yes.
There is feeling, perception, formation, and consciousness, Yes.
Eyes, ears, nose, tongue, body, mind Yes.
Appearances, sounds, smells, taste, touch Yes.
Love, grief, praise, gratitude, Yes.
Relationships and end of relationships, Yes.
Dynamics of sight and mind dynamics Yes.
Dynamics of experience and consciousness Yes.
Beyond experience, Yes.
Knowing and not knowing, Yes.
Ignorance and end of ignorance, Yes.

Old age and death, Yes.
Beyond old age and death, Yes.
Suffering, origin and cessation of suffering, Yes.
Path and Wisdom, Yes.
Attainment and nonattainment, Yes.

Dedicated wisdom beings affirm everything, and they abide in the Presence of what is. They realize all there is is is. They fear and have no fear of fear. They transcend separateness by holding both the one and the many and attain complete inter-being.

All those who appear as wisdom beings of the past, present, and future, by means of profound Presence, fully awaken to unsurpassable, true complete Presence. Therefore, the great mantra of profound Presence, the mantra of great insight and engagement, the supreme mantra of radiance, the mantra that affirms all life and bridges all gaps should be known as truth, since there is no deception. The profound wisdom Presence mantra of affirmation is said in this way:

*Yes! Yes! Now Yes! Always Yes! Yes! Having Gone
Completely Beyond To The Totality, All Hail. Yes!*

## Metaphors for Essence

Essence inspires poets and poetic notions, bringing forth several metaphors. For example, a wave is the immanent nature and the water the transcendent nature of all being. A wave is water and water is a wave.

~

Another metaphor is old-fashioned chocolate pudding, the kind that used to form lumps as it cooked. All being is pudding and the temporary coalescence of that being manifests as lumps. Pudding is the possibility of lumps. Without pudding there are no lumps. Lumps arise, move around a bit as they are cooked, and eventually dissolve into their pudding nature.

## Beyond the Senses

> The thing we tell of can never be found by seeking, yet
> only seekers find it.
>
> —Bayazid Bistami

Essence can be found in the silence. The silence of spiritual aliveness is not of the absence of noise or the stillness of tongues. It is
the listening of the heart to what is beyond all sound and in which
all sound arises.

The path to Essence is not a visible road. Beyond the recognition of
forms and relationships, beyond an intimate knowledge of spiritual practices, beyond the direct experience of Divine states, beyond
all concepts and experience, is Essence. And all is Essence.

*Yes*

## Everything Changes

Using the open, Hosting nature of YES, we not only sense the impermanence of all things, we perceive directly the momentary character
of experience. Everything changes. Everything in the material, sensory world has a beginning, middle, and end. This is good news and
bad news. What we dislike will end. What we like will end.

> Nittai of Arbel said:
> Do not despair because of suffering,
>     for life is suffering.
> Suffering and also joy.
> When life brings you suffering, hurt.
> When life brings you joy, laugh.
> Cling to nothing
>     for all is fleeting.
>     —*Pirke Avot* I:7 as translated by Rabbi Rami Shapiro

## An Open Soul

Indifference to the sublime wonder of life closes the doors of the sacred. No matter what the rational mind may think, the attitude that life is filled with hidden as well as manifest miracles reflects an open, "not knowing" soul. This open aspect of the soul is the basis for the freshness of an engaged heart.

No wonder—we get confused by our concepts.

With wonder—we gain the insight of the heart that can glimpse the Divine.

The YES of wonderment is the gate and touchstone for opening to God as Essence. Wonder aligns us with the sense of the beyond that is immanent in all things—the mystery of Reality. In Wonder we glimpse Essence and open the heart of Essential Wisdom.

That which does the seeing, cannot be seen; that which does the hearing, cannot be heard; and that which does the thinking, cannot be thought.

—The Vedas

## Chapter 3

# YES As Celebration and Service
# God As Creation

Everything that God,
the source and substance of all,
creates in this world
flows naturally from the essence
of God's divine nature.
Creation is not a choice
but a necessity.
It is God's nature
to unfold time and space.
Creation is the extension of God.
Creation is God encountered in time and space.
Creation is the infinite in the garb of the finite.

—*Pirke Avot* VI:11 as translated by Rabbi Rami Shapiro

## CREATION

When we relate to Reality and Essence with YES, we are also affirming the process of Reality which is always changing and becoming. The eternally creative process makes, sustains, and destroys everything in the dance of be-ing and becoming. Creation is continuous, moment to moment, eternally. At this very moment, right now, reading these words, we are being created and re-created and so on. Every moment is always becoming.

~

This wondrous dance of the Divine as Creation inspires awe, gratitude, and praise and gives rise to the impulse to join the dance as participants in the constant Creation of the world. We participate and contribute in this magical generation of life through celebration and service—action that adds value and beauty to the world.

> We might come closer to what is meant in the Bible by the word "God" if we understood it as a verb, and not a verb of simple asserted existence but a verb implying a process accomplishing itself.
>
> —Northrup Frye, *The Great Code*

The creative is the life force—the spirit—that brings each thing into being according to its design—its intelligence. The particular forms of this creative force are often referred to as unseen spirits, angels, or deities. In a sense, everything that exists has its own deity, its own essence nature, and its own Presence. When we release the grip of our materialistic views, we can know these unseen aspects of Reality and meet the dynamic Presence of Reality and Creation.

## Cᴇʟᴇʙʀᴀᴛɪᴏɴ

Yes, things change. Yes, people you love die. Yes, you change and will die. We are a part of this process, this dance of creation. Yᴇs takes us beyond our self concerns to the world in motion. Yᴇs gives us a way of perceiving, relating, and experiencing that expresses our basic dignity and place in the dynamic scheme of things.

As the Divine Creation manifesting through us, we have the capacity to enrich life. Our Creative Presence can join the dance. As we dance we are also danced. Something greater takes over and flows through us.

Yᴇs as Celebration powerfully engages us in this dance with the Divine as Creation. We open our hearts with gratitude, love, and a sense of serving what is greater than ourselves. By offering ourselves and our creations, we nourish the world of meaning and value.

Yᴇs as Celebration expresses gratitude and praise. Yᴇs as Celebration makes the sacred a living, conscious Presence. Yᴇs as Celebration unites our inner and outer worlds, and connects us to forces that shape our lives and the cosmos.

Through celebration we are transported into another state of being where colors are brighter, waves of vital energy awaken our bodies, and the fabric of our connection to the unseen sacred is continually being woven and rewoven.

We celebrate with Yᴇs because it is a natural impulse. We celebrate to give expression to gratitude, praise, joy, wonder, relief, communion, and connection to the larger Presence in the world and the Divine. We celebrate to fill our hearts, our minds, our bodies, our homes, and our communities with the affirmation of life. We celebrate to transcend the ordinary and take flight on the wings of the sacred moment.

Every time we Celebrate life with YES, we are rejoicing. At the same time our very existence is the universe saying YES. Our aliveness is the Divine Celebrating Life through us. The YES that we are is constantly forming and reforming as an expression of the YES that is the Divine as Creation.

Remember the YES of Celebration when you awake in the morning, affirming each day. Radiate YES as you go through your morning routines and throughout your day, as you eat, exercise, work, share with others, relax, and enter sleep. Embrace all the creative powers with YES, allowing their YES to shape and enliven you.

~

When we embrace and surrender ourselves completely to authentic Celebration, we are swept up by a vortex of sight, sound, movement, and feeling into a realm of being which is continually appearing and disappearing, opening and closing, filling and emptying. We experience being graced by the vastness of the Divine, out of time and connected to everyone and all being.

YES as Celebration harnesses the horses of our longing for belonging, our desire to know God and be known in our true nature, our love of life and our impulse to express our deepest feeling. We hitch these horses to our affirmation; our prayers; our meditations; our songs of love, joy, grief, and praise; and our listening to the most profound silence. In Celebration we gain entrance to the splendid world of ecstacy.

## Praise

The Yes of Celebration is fundamentally praise. Praise is the active celebration of the value of life seen in the object of our appreciation. It is the honoring both of what is and of the eternal process of becoming. It is the radiation of uplifting energy. It is the Heart Posture of Applause. It is appreciation, gratitude, and embracing with a large dose of joy.

Praise is an act of connection. Praise refines our sacred emotional capacity and cultivates relationship and inter-being. Praise is an act of reaching out and exposing our heart to the possibility of being touched in our core. Praise is our aliveness expressing value and radiating love. Praise holds both knowing and not knowing with a sense of glorious wonder.

To praise is to become a lover. All love is a form of praise—a willingness to open, be touched, and have loving, valuing energy evoked. To love is to value intensely, wholeheartedly. The various acts of lovemaking are an alchemical art of praising, and, through praising, transforming the ordinary into the extraordinary and sublime. Through love, we transcend our body of reactive habits and create a celebrational body of joy and wisdom energy.

## Grief as Praise

The YES of grief is a form of praise. Consciously celebrating the value of what we have lost and honoring the aliveness of the pain deepens our sacred sensibilities and intensifies our Presence with the Creative. Our heart is broken so that we can expand our embrace and transcend our self-preoccupations.

> Everything praises God. Darkness, privations,
> defects, evil too praise God and bless God.
> —Meister Eckhart

When we, individually and collectively, do not grieve the losses and tragedies of our lives and in the world, we cannot grow. Incomplete grieving denies the Creative in life and forms reactive habits and homeless, hungry inner ghosts that feed on the life energy of our health, work, and relationships. These hungry ghosts appear as obsessions, compulsions, addictions, alienation, and a haunting sense of neediness. They will devour our dearest relationships and corrupt our best intentions.

The YES of authentic praise as Love turns lead into gold. Yet, if it is not heartfelt, it can turn everything and anything, even gold, into lead.

Praise evokes an uplifting quality, an upward movement of energy. It makes events sacred. Praise takes us beyond ourselves and gets us to attend to what is beyond.

Oh, tell us, poet, what it is you do?
>I praise.

But in the midst of death and violent turmoil,
what helps you endure and how do you take it in?
>I praise.

And that which nameless is, beyond —
how do you poets raise that, invoke the unnameable?
>I praise.

What right have you to pose in any guise,
wear any mask, and still remain true?
>I praise.

—and that the stillness and the turbulence,
like star and storm, know and acknowledge you?
>Because I praise.

>—Rainer Maria Rilke as translated by M.L.

## Collective Celebration

When we celebrate in community, our dedication, actions, and embodiment are amplified by the collective participation and alignment of intention and energy. As we celebrate, we are being celebrated, being worked by the larger whole in which everything can merge into the process and experience of celebration.

The YES of collective Celebration aligns hearts and minds, allowing us to give ourselves to something larger and to each other. In collective celebration, as in group worship and meditation, we not only sit, stand, sing, and dance side by side, but we witness each other, share our life energy, and are inspired and supported by the engagement of those around us.

*Yes*

Celebration through singing, chanting, toning, praising, gesturing, and meditating awakens our capacity for vision of the invisible world. Celebration brings unseen spirits to life, investing them with our energy so that they may in turn embody their energy in us. The YES of Celebration calls forth healing, loving, and wisdom qualities for the benefit of ourselves, others, and the world.

## Embodiment

As we mature in our celebrational capacity, we find our own voice, our authentic movements, and our sacred vision. We align these with those of others in the creation of a temple of praise that can invite and contain the vastness and power of sacred energies. To hold these Presences and energies with our Yes requires our unreserved Presence—our wholehearted intention, simultaneous concentration and surrender, open attention, and relaxation into stillness and silence—to manifest the rich paradox that is life.

In celebrations and the enactment of chants, stories, prayers, blessings, and songs, it is the intent and meaning of the words that directs our attention and it is the activity itself which mobilizes and evokes the actual energy of embodiment. We build our capacity for Creative Presence and strengthen the Yes of our heart.

## Ritual

Rituals are a way to bring all the elements of celebration together. The word "ritual" comes from *ritus*, Latin meaning "to fit together." Ritual weaves the fragments of our lives, individually and collectively, into a vital fabric of meaning. Ritual takes us beyond our daily pressures and self concerns into Reality, Essence, Wisdom, and the Creative. Ritual is action that connects us and expresses our relationship to both the seen and unseen worlds, including the sacred qualities and energies of the Divine in all aspects.

Sacred rituals are a form of YES and celebrate the spiritual. Sacred ceremonies affirm, praise, supplicate, evoke, invoke, and activate the energies and qualities of Creation. They align us with the Creative to give direction to our work, our relationships, and our growth. They are a regular way of binding the stability of collective form with the spontaneity of the individual heart in affirmation and Celebration.

Our Celebration blesses the Creative and is blessed by the Creative. The power of our aliveness intensifies in this mutual exchange, and the quickening of the Creative nourishes our being and presence and that of others.

## Beauty

The creation of beauty is another form of affirmation, praise, and celebration. Sacred art wrestles Spirit into matter and becomes a medium for the qualities of Creation and of Wisdom. Visual art, music, chanting, dance, and poetry have the potential to evoke our most profound nature, inspire us with awe, and bring the sacred energies to life. Mystical art reveals multiple dimensions of Reality, meaning, and Being. Working through the sensory dimension, authentic sacred art transmits and brings together all dimensions of awareness.

Beauty strikes a deep chord in our being that resonates with awe and YES. The creation and witnessing of beauty evokes a loving YES, engagement, and Presence. Beauty conveys a glimpse of the boundless radiance of the Divine. The YES of sacred art opens a door to the beauty of aliveness.

## AFFIRMING ACTION

By "affirming action" I mean all the different kinds of conscious action done with a sense of Presence and intended to create benefit. These range from personal acts of generosity, support, teaching, and celebration, to organized service, work on a job, and community and political activity aimed at insuring justice and creating a better society.

Affirming action places us in the world, belonging to the community of humanity and life in all its forms. It gives purpose and meaning to our lives. In the YES of action we live the meaning. When we act from YES of Presence, our actions are invested with the spirit of love, wisdom, and peace. The action is infused with the qualities of conscious Presence of the actor.

The intention to create benefit must be wedded to effort and skill. Without effort there is only hollow sentiment. Without skill effort may be misdirected and not realize our intention. Our YES to the Creative is realized through our actions. We make ourselves servants of love, compassion, and justice to affirm the Divine possibilities in ourselves, others, and the world. Caring and service awaken and nourish our basic humanity.

## A Welcoming Host

According to the *American Heritage Dictionary*: the Indo-European root of the words "host," "hospice," and "hospital" is *ghosti*, which is also the root for the word "guest" and meant "stranger" as well. Thus host, guest, and stranger are all people "with whom one has reciprocal duties of hospitality."

Affirming action of YES begins with the sense of being a Hosting Presence. As a "host," we welcome others into our home, which is as much our heart as our physical space. We offer to nourish them and share what is ours, provide them with a refuge in which to heal and to make connection with the sacred, engage them in a mutual dance of conversation, learning and growing, and create a mutual "home" of belonging and sacred Presence.

When we extend hospitality to others or when we receive the hospitality of others, we connect to the Divine through each other and have a home in the world. It is through this connection that we find the Divine in ourselves. The alternative cuts us off from others and thus from ourselves, losing the communion with life and with God. In the denial of hospitality to others, we deny life. Greeting the other with the Hosting YES affirms both of us, affirms the relationship, and affirms life.

This hosting is like the parenting impulse in which we actively care about and for the well-being of our child—loving, respecting, nourishing, protecting, and transmitting what is of value through our actions and our Presence to another, precious, miraculous creation of the life force.

## Guests, Strangers

At Passover, the Jewish festival celebrating the freedom from slavery in Egypt, a place is always set for Elijah who could show up in the form of a stranger.

In the practice of hospitality as service, we share the goods of the earth and the energies of life with another fellow creature and we accept the stranger and guest into our life. This affirmative act of hospitality constitutes the very essence of an open, grateful, and loving relationship with God as Creation. By giving generously of what we have received to the stranger, we offer to God our thanksgiving for the gift of life and the fruits that have blessed us. The other person is an opportunity to enter into communion with God as Creation.

Even if not physically present, a stranger or guest occupies a special place in the circle of family, household, and community. The stranger is accepted as a visitation of God, of Christ, of Zeus, or some Divine Being. The sacred character of the guest derives from our understanding that we share the same situation. We are all guests of the earth, of God, of life, partaking in the fruits of creation.

## Responsibility

Along with our affirmation of what is, we have the impulse to improve our situation, the lives of others, and the conditions in the world. Our responsibility is to create benefit out of what is. It is not about blame for the past or looking for who else created what is. Our YES simply acknowledges that conditions are what they are no matter how they got that way or who played a part in the process. Understanding how things got to be the way they are may be useful for creating beneficial change; but blame, regret, resentment, and lament all keep us trapped in our reactive habit body and do nothing to improve the world. To take responsibility is to create benefit out of the conditions of life as it is.

> A Hasid asked his Rebbe: "How can I best serve God?" expecting to hear a profound and esoteric answer. The Rebbe replied: "One can best serve God with whatever one is doing at the moment."
>
> —Hasidic Teaching

## The Connection of Compassion

> Christ has no body now on earth but yours,
> no hands but yours, no feet but yours,
> Yours are the eyes through which to look out with
> Christ's compassion to the world;
> Yours are the feet with which he is to go about doing
> good;
> Yours are the hands with which he is to bless men now.
> —St. Teresa of Avila

In Presence with Reality and Creation, we are aware of the inter-being and interconnectedness of all people and creatures. In addition we know that we all share impermanence, vulnerability, and mortality in our physical form.

We also know that we all share the eternal radiance of life, the life force that is the Divine. These are the ingredients of compassion. Compassion is the natural response of an open heart. Compassion does not mean pity or sympathy for the pain of others. In compassion we are present with the pain of others and care for them with the heartfelt desire to bring about their happiness.

For Buddha, who spoke Pali, the word for compassion was *metta*, which is derived from *mitta* (friend). Compassion in Buddhism involves "true friendliness." We can serve by feeding, housing, and tending to starving and homeless people and/or we can serve by teaching, parenting, counseling, and being a true friend to people who are fearful, reactive, and addicted in their mental/emotional lives.

Affirming action of YES works to create a society of support for the physical, mental/emotional, and spiritual well-being of all members. We treat all people and living beings as part of our family.

The wisdom of compassion—the clarity about our nature, about Reality, and about the basic confusion of suffering—comes from opening ourselves wholeheartedly to the unknown with YES and developing unshakable knowledge of our freedom and dedication. The essential nature of compassion is revealed and developed as we embrace all experiences and all living beings with YES. Compassion shares our aliveness in building a more humane world.

## Service

> I slept and dreamt that life was joy. I awoke and saw
> that life was service. I acted and behold, service was
> joy.
>
> —Rabindranath Tagore

Yes to all the kinds of work and activity we do reflects a Heart Posture of Service. The Heart Posture of Service affirms the value of our actions. The benefit may be for others, the world, or God. The generosity of giving love, peace, joy, and wisdom enhances the reservoir of these qualities in the world. As we give, so are we receiving. The more we give, the more we live in a world of love from which we are also receiving.

~

Random acts of kindness are a spontaneous expression of our Yes as a spark of God as Creation. In Yes our spiritual aliveness sees that we are meeting God in everyone we serve and everything we do that makes ourselves and others more awake.

> Put your heart, mind, intellect and soul even to your
> smallest acts. This is the secret of success.
>
> —Swami Sivananda

In the Yes of affirming action there is no sense of helper and helped, only the engagement in a relationship. We do not define another person as needy and ourselves as resourceful. The other person is a full living being with loves, hopes, fears, joys, pains, and resources whom we meet with our loves, hopes, fears, joys, pains, and resources. We mutually engage in a human interaction in which the actions we take become a vehicle for connecting and expressing our reciprocal relationship. Their needs may be what gets our attention and this does not diminish them. A need simply is the opening for the relationship to manifest. Celebrations, mutual crisis, shared interests, and mutual endeavors are also openings to relate and dance together.

Affirming action evokes the gratitude for the opportunity and capacity to give of ourselves. Service becomes a way of giving thanks for what we have received. Service itself brings more inner treasures, growing our gratitude and leading to more caring and service.

## *Affirming the Outcome*

With each action, affirm the result with YES, even if it is not what you intended or would want. The result simply is and responsibility now means creating benefit from that. We affirm the outcome with our Hosting Presence in YES and act from there.

There is an old Yiddish proverb that goes: "If you want to give God a good laugh, tell God your plans." In the process of taking responsibility, learning from the results creates value in itself and gives us more skill and choices for the future.

Everything we do creates a kind of death, a tear or hole in the fabric of life that must be repaired. This is the destruction of what is to make room to create what is becoming. This is not a violation, but a natural process of life that carries with it responsibility—to create benefit from what has been destroyed in the process of creating something new.

## Recycle

Every activity that creates something new leaves waste. If we regard it as simply of no value, we lose our connection to it, diminishing our personal world and the collective world. This alienation then haunts both us and what we have created. It becomes like a homeless spirit that will keep seeking a way back into our heart. If not embraced as a friend and ally, then it will return as a stranger and potential enemy. That waste must be used in a responsible way by finding a practical role for it or by using it to create something of beauty that is dedicated to the sacred. We turn the remains of creation into an offering to the Divine to keep the world intact.

## Contribute

Even when we do something for ourselves we can hold the perspective that we are dedicating the benefits we experience to helping others and awakening their spiritual aliveness. We can extend this affirmation of our connection to others by offering all the benefits we gain to the happiness, growth, and freedom of all living beings.

The YES of contribution affirms both the value of the world and of ourselves. Conscious service not only contributes to others but affirms our own growth in wisdom and our expanding experience of connection as part of the larger story of life. We become motivated in part by the enjoyment of contributing as much good to the world as possible.

Conscious livelihood includes not only the goods and services we receive but all that nourishes our aliveness. The energy of aliveness flourishes on making a contribution. It is through our contributions that we make life worth living and create a legacy.

## We Are the Environment for Others

We are the environment that others experience. Our very presence contributes to the world of others. In conscious Presence and affirmative action we create a welcoming, awakening, and supportive environment.

Part of our challenge in the Yᴇꜱ of affirming action is to integrate our embracing, hosting Presence with our desire to improve the conditions of others. We want to translate the equality we see in all people as manifestations of God as Reality and as Creation into the social/material conditions in the world. We want to bring the quality of consciousness to all actions to create an environment for others to be conscious.

## The Golden Fortune

This is an adaptation of a story of the same name found in *Tales of the Dervishes* by Idries Shah.

~

In another time and another place, that is also here and now, lived a merchant named Abdul Malik. He was known far and wide as an exceptionally good man. From his enormous fortune, he gave generously to charity and fed the poor.

One day as he prayed, Abdul Malik reflected upon his good fortune and the joy he felt at being able to be of service to others. It also occurred to him that he was simply giving away a small portion of what he had and that the needs of the poor and the ill were great; and that his good feelings that flowed from his generosity far exceeded the cost of his sacrifice. As soon as these thoughts arose in his mind, he realized that he really wanted to give away every penny for the good of humankind simply because the need existed.

And he did so. Abdul Malik divested himself of all his possessions and retired to a small house to face whatever life might have in store for him. As Abdul Malik sat meditation, a strange figure seemed to rise from the floor. A man, dressed in a colorful robe of a mysterious dervish, took shape before his very eyes.

"O Abdul Malik, generous man of Khorasan!" sang the apparition in a voice from beyond this world. "I am your authentic self, which has now become almost fully realized because you have done something truly generous beyond any of your previous acts. Because you were able to part with your fortune with an open heart absent of thoughts of personal satisfaction, I am rewarding you from the real source of wealth.

"In future, I will appear before you every day. Strike me and my image will turn into gold. You will be able to take from this golden image as much as you may wish. Do not fear that you will harm me, because whatever you take will be replaced from the endless source of all endowments."

With that, he disappeared. Abdul Malik sat in wonder and gratitude.

The very next morning a friend named Bay-Akal came to see how Abdul Malik was doing. The two friends were having tea when the specter of the dervish began to manifest itself. Bay-Akal was dumbstruck as the mysterious dervish took full form. He was even more amazed when Abdul Malik struck the radiant apparition with a stick, and the figure fell to the ground, transformed into gold. Abdul Malik took a small part of the treasure for his own needs, gave some gold to his guest, and instructed Bay-Akal to distribute the greater portion to the poor and the infirm.

Now Bay-Akal, not knowing what had gone before, started to think of ways he could perform a similar wonder. He knew that dervishes had strange powers. He concluded that among their remarkable features was the transformation into gold when beaten.

So he arranged for a great feast and invited all the dervishes in the province to come and dine with him. On the appointed day, when the dervishes had had their fill of the delights of the banquet, Bay-Akal took up an iron bar and began to thrash every dervish within his reach until they lay battered and broken on the ground.

The remaining dervishes seized Bay-Akal and took him to the local judge. They told the magistrate of the sudden, unprovoked attack. They carried their wounded comrades into the court as evidence and for further testimony. Bay-Akal was very confused. He told the court what he had seen at Abdul Malik's house and exclaimed that he was simply trying to replicate such a rewarding trick.

Abdul Malik was summoned. He was unsure what to reveal or what could be understood about such mysterious wonders. On the way to the court his golden self whispered in his ear what to say.

"May it please the court," Abdul Malik began, "this man is indeed a friend of mine and I cannot explain his insane behavior. His story does not correspond with my own experience of what happened in my house. I have never assaulted anybody's flesh or sought to harm them for my own gain."

Bay-Akal was taken to a cell until he could become calm and was no longer preoccupied with obtaining gain at the expense of others. The dervishes recovered almost at once, through inner healing methods known only to themselves. And nobody believed the astonishing story of Bay-Akal, for the possibility of a man who becomes a golden statue to be broken daily seemed beyond comprehension.

For many years, until he joined his forefathers beyond this life, Abdul Malik continued to break the image which was himself, and to distribute its treasures, which was himself, to all those whom he could help.

## Chapter 4
## Yes As Love
## God As Beloved

The following is my version of an Elijah de Vidas story from *Reishit Chokhmah*, as told by Rabbi Isaac of Akko.

~

One day a princess emerged from the bathhouse and a man who was sitting there sighed a deep sigh and said, "Oh that someone would let me make love to her!" Whereupon the princess replied, "In the cemetery, but not here!" Hearing this, he was overjoyed because he thought she meant for him to go to the graveyard and wait for her there. Then she would come to him and they would experience all the delight of rapturous lovemaking. But this was not her intention at all, saying what she did to dismiss him, who was so unrefined and gross, from her royal presence.

So the man rose and went to the cemetery. He waited there, devoting all his thoughts to her, continually imagining her body, her smile, and her delicate features. Out of his great desire for her, he left behind thoughts of superficial and ordinary things, concentrating instead on the princess and her beauty. In this way he waited, day and night, in the graveyard. In this home for the dead, he ate and drank and slept. Each day he thought, if she doesn't come today, she must be delayed and will surely come tomorrow. And so he waited and concentrated for a very long time.

He increasingly divorced himself from everyday sensual and material concerns. His concentration of all his thoughts and feelings on one thing grew stronger and more continuous. Gradually yet surely his concentration and his all-encompassing longing transformed him. His devotion and his love became so intense that he surrendered everything else, even the woman herself. And thus, transcending all sensual desire, he knew only his longing for the Divine.

He held to his love of God so openly and completely that he became a blessed servant and holy man. Through his connection to the Divine, his prayers were heard and were effective for all those who passed on foot and sought his blessings. All kinds of people, royal and ordinary, would stop to receive his blessing. His loving presence became an inspiration for people far and wide. Simply hearing about this great lover would immediately tap their longings, open their hearts, and connect them to the source of all love, God.

## SOUL AS LOVER

YES is the affirmative manifestation of the soul as lover. The heart affirmation of YES radiates the love in the soul for the Beloved—God.

~

The dimension of our being that makes dancing with Grace—the Divine—possible is the soul. The soul is a lover, bringing the qualities of the Divine to life in all dimensions of being. The soul has the Beloved inside and the Beloved inside recognizes the Beloved in all existence. The soul seeks the Beloved (God) and the experiential union with all that is. The soul lives and grows through conscious love and retreats from disinterest, indifference, and deadening reactive habit. The natural impulse of the soul is to connect—to love—and we manifest that love through our participation and contributions.

Soul is both a source of love and a creation as manifestation of love. The source is not only the Beloved, but also the Reality, Essence, Creation, and Wisdom aspects of the Divine.

*Yes*

The soul is a lover of life as a way of embracing Reality; a lover of being as a way of opening to Essence; a lover of becoming, manifesting, creating beauty, and having an impact as a way of expressing Creation; and a lover of learning as a way of consciously knowing, growing, and integrating all faces of God in Wisdom. To be happy and free is to be totally in love without reservation. Love is a way of Being. The soul we create is the contribution we make in life through our actions and relationships.

Love is aliveness expressing its Divine nature. Interest is love. Positive intent is love. Worship is a form of love. What we worship we give our loving energy to. Caring is the activity of love making personal connection to what we experience. From that caring we create personal meaning. Meaning is our image of the Beloved and the place we give people, experiences, things, and nature in our inner world of kinship.

> God's most effective, strongest creation is love.
>
> —Bahaiddin, Rumi's father

*Yes*

## A Sacred Lover

The sacred is the vital, loving energy of all things. For us to know the sacred, we must first know that it exists, then recognize it, meet it, dance with it, and make love with it. To mature is to grow into the full meaning and possibilities of being a sacred lover. To be a lover is to hold the Beloved in our heart. Mature love holds no illusions and embraces the Beloved unconditionally, opening to being worked by the love of the Beloved.

> To be ignorant of love's embrace is to be a bird without wings.
>
> —M.L.

When we take the surface of the material world to be our lover, we experience conditional relationships and shallow emotional love. When we love the sacred in any dimension of being, we are connecting with God.

The path of YES as Love is the way of direct love and direct inner experience. Surrender, gratitude, and praise are the tools of love that open the gate of love to the Heart Posture of Love.

## Our True Beloved

We master the skills of love and we mature into being a lover. In mature love we realize that God is Love itself (Beloved) in all splendor (Reality), openness and immanence (Essence), vitality and beauty (Creation), and conscious inclusiveness (Wisdom).

For each aspect of God, there is a possible dance with our soul. The question challenging us is: Are our eyes open to God or is our vision obscured by reactive habits and self preoccupation? As lovers, are we seeing the sacred in all dimensions of life, or are we relating only to the surface of sensory experience, becoming identified with and attached to the superficial aspects of the material world, of our thoughts, and of our feelings? The work of a lover is to discover our true Beloved beyond our confused, reactive, emotional substitutes. Spiritual work is opening the inner eyes of wisdom to guide us in the dance of life, with Grace showing up as our partner.

The Beloved is calling to us everywhere all the time. All hear the call with their heart but few pause to listen and fewer still know how to listen. Our very aliveness and longing are notes in the love song of the Beloved inviting us to dance with the sacred.

*Yes*

## Ecstasy

> You may try a hundred things, but love alone will release
> you from yourself. So never flee from love—not even
> from love in an earthly guise—for it is a preparation
> for the supreme Truth. How will you ever read the Koran
> without first learning the alphabet?
>
> —Jami

As we combine our attention, hosting Presence, and conscious engagement, the energy of creation arises out of the moment. This union of Grace and self, of love and desire, of action with Divine harmony, of energy and openness, gives rise to a quality of ecstasy.

This ecstasy of being is not a concept or an emotion. It is not something explosive or excited. It is an inner fire that is radiant and sweet. All of us have experienced moments of ecstasy, listening to music, gazing at the sunset, viewing the vastness of the Grand Canyon, or the simple blissful awe of a birth. In these moments we dissolve into the pure love of life, resting in Grace with an open heart.

When we experience this ecstasy, we develop an attitude that we will not settle for anything less in life. The beauty of it invites us and the energy propels us. However, we must build ourselves as a container for it. Unless our body/mind and our attention are trained, the energy can lead to emotional excitation, mental grandiosity, and a kind of manic obsession that eventually leads to a crash and depression.

Developing YES as Love as a Heart Posture builds a container for Love in our being. Having the capacity to work with the flow of ecstatic aliveness, we make our lives a work of art, with every breath another stroke of color, every word a line, every action a form, and every encounter another painting. We transform the canvas of the world into a landscape of rich colors and multiple perspectives—into a vibrant portrait of the soul.

~

The ardor of ecstasy, *hitlahavut* in Hebrew—the inflaming, is the fire that burns away superficial false identities and habits and the light that reveals the way to the Beloved. This fiery light of love reveals the loving nature of the world and unlocks the meaning of life by infusing everything with the significance of love.

> A seeker went to ask a sage for guidance on the Sufi way. The sage counseled, "If you have never trodden the path of love, go away and fall in love; then come back and see us."
>
> —Jami

*Yes*

## Sacred Marriage

In our love, we sense that God is the Ocean of Being and that we are waves on the surface of that boundless ocean. As waves we hold contradictory attitudes. We feel the life force of the Beloved that gave rise to our existence. At the same time, we are wholly within the grasp of dynamics which will ultimately collapse our wave in the oceanic ground of being out of which we came and from which we never really separated ourselves.

> I read the words of St. John: "Not that we love God, but that He loved us"... Through all these years I had thought that I had been seeking God. The presence which had appeared to me beneath the forms of nature that day at school; the beauty which I had found in the poets; the truth which philosophy had opened to me; and finally the revelation of Christianity; all these had seemed to be steps on my way of ascent towards God. Now I suddenly saw that all the time it was not I who had been seeking God, but God who had been seeking me. I had made myself the centre of my own existence and had my back turned to God.... Yet always I had had the feeling that in love the secret of life was to be found. And so I felt that love take possession of my soul. It was as though a wave of love flowed over me, a love as real and personal as any human love could be, and yet infinitely transcending all human limitations. It invaded my being and seemed to fill not only my soul but also my body.
>
> —Bebe Griffiths, *The Golden String*

Only to the extent that we are capable of letting the boundless love of the Beloved flow through and from us can we realize our potential as Lovers. Only when we have the capacity to completely lose ourselves—lose our reactive habit body and identity—in love can we experience the true Sacred Marriage.

Let the Beloved kiss me with the kisses of God's mouth.

—Song of Songs 1:2

*Yes*

## Living in Love

> Love makes us speak; love makes us moan; love makes
> us die; love brings us to life; love makes us drunk and
> bewildered; it sometimes makes one a king. Love and
> the lover have no rigid doctrine. Whichever direction the
> lover takes, he turns toward his beloved. Wherever he
> may be, he is with his beloved. Wherever he goes, he
> goes with his beloved. He cannot do anything, cannot
> survive for even one moment, without his beloved. He
> constantly recalls his beloved, as his beloved remem-
> bers him. Lover and beloved, rememberer and
> remembered, are ever in each other's company, always
> together.
>
> —Sheikh Muzaffer

When we love with the ecstasy of our spiritual aliveness, we sense
the love that suffuses every dimension of life—spiritual and material. Love becomes the Reality within which we live, hosted by the
Beloved. When we are in the rapture of Love, loving the Beloved
and being loved by the Beloved, the ordinary becomes golden and
the habitual is eternally new.

~

The experience of total openness, wonder, and the rapture of sacred
love all result in a loss of ordinary self. Love and spiritual ecstasy
bring down the walls of the reactive, assumed self and offer us greater
sensitivity to each experience and to the world around us.

In Divine Love, we are willing to die to become one with the
Beloved, reborn in Glory. As we meditate, pray, or simply give
homage, we prepare to die from the intensity of our devotion.

## Devotion

When we awaken to the possibility of a more authentic life and the radiance of the Divine in the universe, our heart is cracked open. The reactive self of the habit body is burned alive by the flames of the Divine spark that had been hidden. The heat of that fire provides the energy and the ashes the material from which we reemerge into a sacred world of reawakened wonder, unimpeded love, and fresh clarity. Devotion immerses us in the act of loving with a willingness to unconditionally serve the Sacred. It dissolves the identities of self, binding us wholly to the Sacred Lover. Devotion to the Beloved in the path of Love requires the absolute and complete surrender of who we think and feel we are, directing our attention to Grace.

The heartbreak of YES as Love breaks us down and opens us over and over again with the beauty, the majesty, and the pain of ecstatic love, that cannot be grasped or contained.

## Awaken to Bliss

> You only need smell the wine
> For vision to flame from each void—
> Such flames from wine's aroma!
> Imagine if you were the wine.
>
> —Rumi

Just as sperm and egg have no clue about the world of sky, sun, stars, mountains, rivers, and trees, so we are ignorant of the Divine world of bliss. Only after the sperm and egg combine and grow through the painful loss of the womb and the birth into a vaster world, can we know another Reality and move toward the full Reality of God. This Reality can only be seen with the clear eyes of an awakened heart.

Before our heart can awaken, it must open. And before it can open, it must break. The cries of a broken heart are the prayers for transformation and hunger pains for Divine renewal. This destruction of the old self—sometimes seriously resisted, often hilariously embraced—happens in bursts, in challenges, in breakdowns, in temptations, in desolation, and in simple delights. Eventually we surrender, offering ourselves totally to the Beloved.

In a sense, the Beloved in our heart recognizes the Beloved that recognizes the Beloved in us. The spiritual discipline of becoming clear, harmonizing all aspects of our being, and cultivating an open, loving, and generous heart creates a mirror in which the loving nature of all Being is reflected with beauty.

> A human being must be born twice. Once from the mother, and again from the body and one's own existence. The body is like an egg, and the essence of a person must become a bird in that egg through the

warmth of love, and then the essence can escape from the body and glory in the eternal world of the soul beyond time and space.

—Sultan Walad

## Freedom

The power of Divine Love transforms our vision from ordinary sight to the perception of love everywhere in everything. We lose our inhibitions of reaction in order to dance openly with the exuberant energy of the Beloved. The following is a Sufi story.

~

A great monarch loved a slave immensely and wanted to know if the slave really reciprocated the love. So, into a room heaped with treasures of all kinds, including jewels and deeds to vast estates, all the slaves were summoned and told, "You are free. Whatever you want in this room, you can take." The slaves could hardly believe their luck. They ran about the large hall cramming as much as they could into their pockets, and then scampered off, yowling, hollering, and clapping their hands. But the slave whom the great monarch loved did not move during the entire time. When the room was empty, the slave walked quietly over to the monarch and stood there with eyes full of love. The monarch said, "What do you want?" And the slave replied, "I want you. Just you." And the great monarch said to the slave, "Because all you want is me, you are completely free and all that I possess is yours."

### Love Blossoms

In Love, the soul tries to wed every moment, every breath, every thought, every feeling to the Radiance of the Beloved. This takes enormous effort with incredible determination and stamina and is also intensely beautiful and enlivening.In this relationship we become drunk with the elixir of love and are prepared to drown in its vast, fluid embrace.

The words of our prayers and our praises are flowers woven into a bouquet for the Beloved. Each utterance has a soul, a lover that sustains the vibration of our songs and carries them to the home of the Divine.

> In the Ocean of the Heart love opens its mouth
> And gulps down the two worlds like a whale.
>
> Hear from the heart wordless mysteries!
> Understand what cannot be understood!
> In man's stone-dark heart there burns a fire
> That burns all veils to their root and foundation.
> When the veils are burned away, the heart will
> understand completely . . .
> Ancient Love will unfold ever-fresh forms
> In the heart of the Spirit, in the core of the heart.
>
> —Rumi

Love as YES blossoms more beautiful and softer than flowers, even sweeter than flowing honey, more radiant than the sun, more vigorous than a bounding antelope, more intimate than skin, more patient than a rock, more insistent than a heartbeat, more embracing than a womb, and joyful beyond imagination and longing.

*True Desires*

> Light the incense!
> You have to burn to be fragrant
> To scent the whole house
> You have to burn to the ground.

—Rumi

In this journey we seek the Beloved and in the process discover our true self. The following is a Hasidic story that is found in many traditions around the world:

A peasant who lived in Lublin, dreamed of a very great treasure. In the vivid dream, under a tree in a courtyard could be seen a heap of radiant jewels and an elderly person sitting beside the tree. Even the address of the house of this treasure was apparent—number 3 River Street in Krakow. Having learned enough to trust dreams, the peasant set off on the long, arduous journey to Krakow. One day— it may have been years later—the peasant came to the doorway of the courtyard and entered with great anticipation. Sure enough, sitting beside the tree was the elderly person from the dream.

The peasant said, "I had a dream many years ago, and in the dream I saw you sitting exactly where you are now and I saw this great treasure. I have come to tell you my dream and to claim the treasure that was revealed to me." The old sage smiled, embraced the peasant and said, "How strange, I had a dream last night that under the cooking fire in a poor house in Lublin there was the greatest treasure I have ever seen." At that moment, the peasant saw that what had been sought for all those years was really at home. The peasant made the journey home and in the hearth of the heart was the treasure—all along at the very core of life.

## *Heart of the Believer*

Eventually we experience the Divine marriage all the way down to the cellular level of our bodies and our being. We ascend to the Radiance of the Beloved and the Radiance of the Beloved descends to meet us filling our body, heart, and mind. Then we flower, radiating Love and being held endlessly in the embrace of Love.

The alchemical power of YES as Love—holy possession—transforms the basis of our life, revealing the radiant nature of the soul.

In Islam, one who knows the Soul as Lover and the Path of YES as Love is referred to as a "believer." To believe is to Love God as Beloved. In the Koran it says of the Beloved: "I cannot fit into my heavens or into my earth but I fit into the heart of my believing servant."

"The heart of the believer is the place of the revelation of God. The heart of the believer is the throne of God. The heart of the believer is the mirror of God."

*Yes*

## Chapter 5

# Yes As Learning and Dedication
# God As Wisdom

There is a certain wisdom which we preach among the spiritually mature. It is not a wisdom of this age nor of the leaders of this age, who will all die and become nothing. We preach the wisdom of God, mysterious and hidden, which was foreordained by God before all ages for our glory, a wisdom that none of the leaders of this age have ever known.

—I Cor. 2:6–8

The reality of the holy can only be grasped from the standpoint of the mystery. Then one sees that the holy is not a segregated, isolated sphere of Being, but signifies the realm open to all spheres, in which they can alone find fulfillment. The face of the holy is not turned away from but towards the profane; it does not want to hover over the profane but to take it up into itself. "The mysteries always teach us to combine the holy with the profane." The strict division between them has its place not in the character and attitude of the holy but in those of the profane; it is the profane which makes a fundamental and unsurmountable division between itself and the holy, and on the other side the inadequate "usual" holiness consists in being separate from the profane, whereas the perfectly holy thinks and wills nothing but unity. The contradictions between the spheres of the holy and the profane exist only in the subjectivity of man who has not yet attained to spiritual unity and is unable, with his limited powers of understanding, to mediate between the two. In reality the main purpose of life is to raise everything that is profane to the level of the holy.

—Martin Buber, *On Zion*

It is not peace we seek but meaning. . . . It is not meaning that we need but sight.

—Lawrence Durrell

## Dedicated to Sacred Wisdom

What a wonderful mystery life is. We are surrounded by mystery, surrounded by the unknown beyond our vision, the unknown beneath our skin, the unknown between our thoughts, the unknown of being itself. From this unknown springs life, activity, and wonder. From the mystery arises our world of experience, meaning, and beauty.

Yes in Presence has the characteristic of establishing an open, hosting relationship with this mystery—with everything that arises. Some refer to this as a process of coming home, others as developing a friendly, intimate, direct relationship to ourselves, our minds, and the world, and still others as welcoming the unseen, animating forces which inhabit the inner landscape and the outer cosmos.

In dedication to Presence, Truth, and Service we are initiated into the Divine Wisdom that is "mysterious and hidden."

Whereas the soul, through our sense of being, draws power and nourishment from experience, our vanity, through our personality, wishes to maintain power over experience and to control events and their consequences to meet its own perceived needs. To nourish the sacred dimensions of our being through lived experience requires that we are fully present and that we sense both the sacred and sensory dimensions of the moment. This is accomplished by interrupting the habitual patterns of reaction and gaining clarity about who we are and what our true nature is.

The clarity we are talking about here has many aspects. The first involves slowing thought patterns so we can redirect and consciously use our attention. The second is relaxing beyond the agitation and tension of emotions and seeing beyond the filters that emotions and moods place in front of our lens of perception. From these first two processes, we begin to settle into a more open Heart Posture in relation to what is occurring. We become clear in Yes.

～

Essentially, in our Dedication to Wisdom we use everything to awaken our aliveness with clarity and authenticity. In the YES of Dedication we have the direct and intuitive experience of Reality, moment to moment, and manifest this in the world as a beneficial Presence in our relationships, our work, and our community. YES is a path which acquaints our mind with our wisdom nature and cultivates the wisdom qualities of that essential nature as an authentic expression of our aliveness.

## Our Self-Sense

In order to develop clarity we need to work from our self-sense. Our self-sense is an awareness that is God as Wisdom manifesting through each of us. This self-sense is the starting place for all conscious work. It is not the identity, an idea about what we are, but the sense that there is someone that reads this passage, that eats meals, that has experiences, that learned to walk, that has a body, that has thoughts and emotions, that can notice minute sensations, that can feel the smallest bump on a smooth surface, that can see a landscape thousands of times the size of our eyes, that can imagine being in locations thousands of miles away and even millions of miles out in space, that has a sense of Presence and that can simply "be" without having to be somewhere.

Sacred Wisdom reveals the hidden divinity in confused reactions and makes that hidden nature manifest. Wisdom is not a concept, a belief, or a pretension. It is the natural quality of authentic aliveness that is not trapped in reactive sensory identities. The Spiritual Wisdom we are talking about here is not a special knowledge so much as a way of perceiving, relating, and experiencing.

## Divine Spark

Wisdom is not so much achieved as it is uncovered within the depths of our own being. The path begins with the surface layers of our emotional and psychological reactive habit body that stands between our everyday sense of ourselves and the core of wisdom at the heart of the soul.

By cultivating the inherent wisdom of our Divine nature, we shift our ground of being from distress to creativity, disturbance to balance, suffering to well-being. We use the dynamics of aliveness to align our body, mind, and heart.

When we contact our wisdom nature, we are revealing and tapping the Divine spark that gives life to our being and that is inseparable from the Divine light of all existence. In this experience we are struck with awe at the miraculous nature of our life and of all life.

*Yes*

## Wisdom as Solar System

From the viewpoint of everyday consciousness, we are a planet around which everything else seems to revolve. During the day we may get glimpses of a sun (our wisdom nature), but often the clouds obscure it. At night we have no sense of the sun except by reflection off the moon. Our identity seems to make us special and this consciousness appears to be the most important.

From the point of view of the sun (our wisdom nature), the planets are small and all contained by the sun's energy field. There are many planets which revolve around the sun, not simply the planet of surface thoughts and feelings. The planet of sensations is larger and has a wider, more encompassing orbit. The world of the energy of manifestation is even larger and wider. The world of witness is larger still and its orbit is so wide it encompasses the material, mental, and emotional world.

The entire system, including the sun, is hosted in space, the awareness within which everything arises. This is the transcendent mode of awareness beyond knowing and not knowing, beyond distinction, and beyond all concepts.

## Roots of Dedication

The key to making our lives enduring structures of Wisdom for ourselves and others is dedication. Dedication begins with the thought that all beings have the same innermost Divine, sacred, Essence nature and that the way to open the gift of life is to celebrate it. By freeing ourselves and others from reactive habits and confusions, we can celebrate all life as a flowing, vibrant, loving, radiant Presence. This vision becomes the inspiration and motivation for our dedication. Dedication places our efforts in the context of the larger story of humanity and, as an offering, extends the benefits of our work through the value created for others, which they in turn can pass on.

Dedication deepens the Heart Posture of Openness which arises from the realization of our wisdom nature beyond the material, mental, and emotional habits and attachments of our life. We perceive the shallowness and temporariness of possessions, thoughts, and feelings and the fleeting nature of our comforting experiences through being identified with those things. We cultivate the wisdom qualities that transcend ordinary habits of body and mind.

## A Dedicated Life

The Yes of Dedication is about the shape we give our vitality, our energy of aliveness. It is about the way in which we honor the gift of life, the magnificence of the world, and our connections to family, friends, community, all peoples, and nature.

We are determined to bring all the positive powers and wisdom qualities from our spiritual life into the world through our relationships, our work, and our participation in our community. We hold the vision of a world of happiness, growth, and freedom. We commit ourselves to making that vision a reality through sharing the fruits of our growth as a beneficial Presence and a skillful contributor to all life.

When we are dedicated in life, it naturally follows that we do what is necessary to learn and grow throughout our lives. Dedication brings the soul to life and life to our work, relationships, and play. It transforms tasks from burdens into sacred rites. A dedicated life results in an expanded sense of belonging, happiness, and peace as well as the increasing manifestation of Wisdom in realizing goals. We act from alignment with nature, tapping our creative essence, and encountering the world with freshness, joy, and gratitude.

## Meditation

A training tool for Wisdom is meditation. Yes is a way of meditating. The intimate relationship implicit in the affirmation Yes is reflected in a Tibetan term for meditation, "*sgom*," which literally means "to become familiar." The word "familiar" means "to make like family." The various meditation techniques bring us into an intimate relationship with our own mind, with others, and with the world. Being present and being familiar is a state of mind.

Yes as meditation trains attention. Attention is one of the true powers of being human. Attention is the energy (activity) of the self-sense. This is the ability to direct the mind and apply the range of energies of our being. Attention is the lens which brings all things into view. It is the self-sense's beacon which reveals the nearest and farthest reaches of the inner world and brings the outer world into intimate relationship with the self-sense.

While it may be easiest to experience a sense of Presence and belonging while sitting quietly in a serene place, this state of mind can be incorporated into every activity and situation, such as working, walking, cooking, eating, listening, and sleeping.

## Conscious Attention

With conscious attention in Yes we become clear; we integrate awareness into our self-sense; we harmonize and align our awareness and our behavior; and we cultivate the beneficial energies of aliveness that have been waiting for our attention. Conscious attention unleashes the great power of spiritual aliveness.

Wisdom brings us home to the realization of our authentic unitive nature—being totally open, boundlessly radiant, and always presencing. This nature is the fundamental awareness out of which all experience arises and passes through, and into which it disappears.

All of this comes from a desire to continuously grow. We need to relate to our hunger for wisdom and the nourishment of the spirit in the persistent way a child seeks the milk of the mother. We are reaching for the nourishment of the Divine Mother.

*Yes*

## GOD AS ETERNAL QUESTION, ALIVENESS AS THE ANSWER

Grace is another way of talking about God. What is Grace? We know Grace through the experience of awe and wonder, through the unknown, through the miraculous nature of life. We know Grace in the smile of an infant, in the fragrance of an Easter lily, in the calling of the loon, and in the peace in our own heart when we open unconditionally to a living moment. We know Grace when we save an injured bird, nurse a newborn, shape a pot on a wheel, sing a song, and offer a helping hand to someone in need. We *know* it, but *what is* Grace?

The answer is that we cannot locate it or define it. It is both a force and the space within which the force manifests all around us and through us. Grace both emanates from all that is to us and emanates from us to all that is.

## Boundless Grace, Boundless God

The sense of Grace moves us beyond our self-centered concerns into the world of the sacred. It is deep-seated, familiar, and close, and is known through intimate witnessing. As we relax into the space of the intimate witness and into the sense of hosting awareness, we see that life expresses itself in each moment as energy, as experience, as action. From the alchemical process of our attention, hosting Presence, and conscious engagement, the energy of creation arises out of the moment. This is the union of Grace and self, of love and desire, of action with Divine harmony, of energy and openness. This is the alchemical marriage.

We must seek the wisdom of Grace everywhere, not simply by going inside. The idea of an inner world that is separate from an outer world is an illusion. The distinction is temporarily useful because we are starting out with the sense of separation. We are simply penetrating the depths of an artificial distinction to experience that at the core all conceptual distinctions dissolve in the wholeness of all that is, in the undivided nature of the Yes of God.

## Who Are You?

The Divine, as Reality, is always presencing, that is, inviting us to be present. The eternal question is will we show up? Will we let our body feel what it feels? Will we let the engagement of our mind openly think what is true now? Will we let the natural connection of the heart relate wholeheartedly? Our unreserved aliveness is the only answer that can meet the Presence.

Who are you?

You must be still and let the silence define you.

The you that can say, is not who you are.

The question beckons you to come home to your place in the scheme of things.

Each moment of your aliveness in Yes is your answer. Yes brings you home.

## Home

When we come home, we rest in our own nature and experience the intimacy of all life. Experience is direct. There is no separation between the experience, what is experienced, and the witnessing self. As we learn to abide in Yᴇs with wonder and gratitude, the remote and seemingly threatening aspects of unknown worlds reveal their hidden vitality and affinity with us. Our thoughts, images, and feelings then simply give expression and articulation to this fundamental relationship that embraces humanity, all living beings, nature, and divinity as one. In the heart of Wisdom there is no real division between me and you, here and there, time and eternity, the human and the Divine. Everywhere is home. Nowhere is home. Yᴇs as hosting welcomes, includes, and supports everything as being home.

~

True love, true meditation, and true prayer is our everyday life lived without hesitation in Yᴇs. It is the power of our aliveness manifesting the sacred in every moment. Spiritual aliveness is the expression of the Divine, as Beloved Reality, through our Presence.

## Inspired by Awe

YES places us in awe. We are present with Reality and Essence experiencing awe in the face of the mystery of the Divine, the mystery of what is beyond and in all things; is all things; creates, maintains, and destroys all things; and inspires our very awe. Being fully present with this tremendous mystery is our connection to the Divine, as Wisdom. Our conscious attention is clarity. Our wholehearted Presence is unconditional love and compassion. Our inclusive Hosting and Embrace are equanimity and peace. Our open, fresh action is Creation. Our Joy taps the Great Bliss. Our undying Gratitude and Praise are Devotion. All these are our Wisdom responding to the Wisdom that is God.

In our openness to the unknown living answer of each moment, we are showing up as the eternal question. Our self-sense, the sense of *I am* beyond our body and any label or name, abides in a state of be-ing and becoming that is free—free from answers, habits, and needs and free to be present, create, and act.

## Bringing It Together

> Wonder is the heart of life,
> beating in the breast of the living.
>
> Do not imagine that you merit wonder—
> only dare to encounter it.
>
> —*Pirke Avot* V:5 as translated by Rabbi Rami Shapiro

In everyday life we tend to sprinkle the dust of ordinariness, routine, and reaction on the world. YES brings the sense of a powerful living Presence to each moment. By meeting the world with our full aliveness, we enrich not only our experience but the world itself. This is what makes life rich, significant, and wondrous. The key is seeing the extraordinary in the ordinary, investing events, objects, activities, people, and experiences with sacred meaning from the core of our being.

YES is a gateway to value. It is like birth and growth. As parents we know the preciousness of an embryo and later the infant. The beauty is in the sense of conceiving, birthing, nurturing, and caring for the child. Letting the child emerge on its own in its own time. In this way we know that an embryo is really a human and we know that it takes time, care, and feelings to bring this miracle to maturity.

∼

When we emotionally and spiritually engage in the world moment to moment we taste the deliciousness of living life beyond the safety of our habits and reactions. We feed ourselves, our community, and the larger world by the beauty of our tears, our celebrations, and our wholehearted quest to create value. When we express not only the feeling but the larger sense of life, we are participating in the making of a world that encourages, supports, and expands life through time.

In YES we care. We create beauty with our living Presence as well as what we make. We nurture and care for what we create as well as all Creation.

## Tap into Presence, Wisdom, God

The fact that Presence is always everywhere is of no use until we realize it through our aliveness. It is like radio waves. They surround us but are of no use to us until channeled and transformed in some way that allows us to receive them.

In the clarity of Presence, we allow God to think, feel, and work in us. Wisdom is the Divine Presence, Essence, and Creation showing up in us as conscious be-ing, opening, and relating. Our conscious self-sense intuits the totality of God and can be dedicated to manifesting this clear intuition even as we cannot understand that totality. In Yes we are present in this intuition as a living aspect of our being.

Beyond conscious attention, it is our love that brings the current of Presence to life. We experience this love in glimpses at times of romantic love. If we sense deeply, we can tap this capacity for love of life in other activities and times. When we intentionally engage in an activity that we love, we bring objects, actions, and relationships to life. We animate the entire situation and practice the art of dedication and the power of Presence.

As we tap the wellspring of energy in our natural way of being and sense of Presence we relate to our entire environment of people, objects, and places with our aliveness. Everything is fresh and sacred, vital and vibrant, we can sense the Presence of Creation in all things.

Love is a state of being within inter-being that affirms all Presence with our Presence. In love we can feel the aliveness of the totality of God that is showing up in us and everyone and everything else. To feel and be this aliveness is love and, in this sense, all love is God.

# Recommended Reading

Barks, Coleman with John Moyne, trans. *The Essential Rumi* (Harper Collins, 1995).

Barks, Coleman, trans. *The Soul of Rumi* (HarperSanFrancisco, 2001).

Barks, Coleman and Robert Bly, trans. *Night and Sleep* (Yellow Moon, 1981).

Benyosef, Simcha and Elijah Ben Moses De Vidas. *The Beginning of Wisdom* (KTAV Publishing, 2001).

Blofeld, John, trans. *The Zen Teaching of Huang Po* (Grove, 1958).

Bly, Robert, trans. and ed. *Selected Poems of Rainer Maria Rilke* (Harper and Row, 1981).

Buber, Martin. *On Zion: The History of an Idea* (T&T Clark, 2000).

Carlebach, Shlomo with Susan Yael Mesinai. *Shlomo's Stories* (Aronson, 1994).

Cleary, Thomas. *The Essential Koran: The Heart of Islam* (HarperSanFrancisco, 1993).

———. *The Ecstasy of Enlightenment: Teachings of Natural Tantra* (Samuel Weiser, 1998).

Eknath, Easwaran. *The Upanishads* (Nilgiri, 1987).

Fox, Matthew. *Breakthrough: Meister Eckhart's Creation Spirituality in New Translation* (Doubleday, 1980).

Frye, Northrup. *The Great Code: The Bible and Literature* (Harvest, 1983).

Griffiths, Bebe. *A New Vision of Reality* (Harper Collins, 1989).

———. *Return to the Center* (Templegate, 1977).

Hanh, Thich Nhat. *Heart of Understanding: Commentaries on the Prajnaparamita Heart Sutra* (Parallax, 1988).

Harvey, Andrew. *The Essential Mystics* (Harper Collins, 1996).

———. *Teachings of Rumi* (Shambhala, 1999).

———. *The Way of Passion* (Frog, Ltd., 1994).

Hixon, Lex. *Coming Home: The Experience of Enlightenment in Sacred Traditions* (Larson, 1995).

Joyce, James. *Ulysses* (Modern Library, 1934).

Kaplan, Aryeh. *Rabbi Nachman's Stories* (Breslov Research Institute, 1983).

Kushner, Lawrence. *Eyes Remade for Wonder* (Jewish Lights, 1998).

———. *The Way Into Jewish Mystical Tradition* (Jewish Lights, 2001).

Lao Tzu. *The Way of Life.* Translated by Witter Bynner. (Perigee, 1944).

Lowenthal, Martin and Lar Short. *Opening the Heart of Compassion: Transform Suffering Through Buddhist Psychology and Practice* (Charles Tuttle, 1993).

Mitchell, Stephen, trans. and ed. *Ahead of All Parting: The Selected Poetry and Prose of Rainer Maria Rilke* (Modern Library, 1995).

———. *A Book of Psalms* (Harper Collins, 1993).

———. *The Essence of Wisdom: Words from the Masters to Illuminate the Spiritual Path* (Broadway, 1998).

Needleman, Jacob. *Money and the Meaning of Life* (Currency Doubleday, 1991).

Schwartz, Howard. *Elijah's Violin and Other Jewish Fairy Tales* (Harper & Row, 1983).

Sells, Michael, trans. and ed. *Early Islamic Mysticism: Sufi, Qur'an, Mi'raj, Poetic and Theological Writings* (Paulist Press, 1996).

Shah, Idries. *Tales of the Dervishes: Teaching-Stories of the Sufi Masters over the Past Thousand Years* (Dutton, 1970).

Shapiro, Rami. *Wisdom of the Jewish Sages: A Modern Reading of Pirke Avot* (Bell Tower, 1993).

DEDICATED LIFE INSTITUTE

*Cultivating Wisdom Presence for Everyday Life*

The Dedicated Life Institute (DLI) supports spiritual exploration and growth and is dedicated to making the essence teachings of many traditions accessible in a western idiom. Incorporating the principles of the mystic way, we promote both recovery of our wisdom ground of being and development of our capacity to use our daily conditions as a means of growth and an opportunity to manifest our true wisdom nature. Our dedication to living as an expression of wisdom serves to encourage both personal and social transformation. Founded by Martin Lowenthal, the Institute offers meditation groups, retreats, workshops, and a home study program.

For more information please contact:
Dedicated Life Institute
53 Westchester Road
Newton, Massachusetts 02458
617-332-4967
Visit our website: *www.dli.org*